My Little Golden Book About
BALTO

By Chip Lovitt
Illustrated by Sophie Allsopp

The editors would like to thank Amy Phillips-Chan, PhD,
Museum Director, Carrie M. McLain Memorial Museum,
for her assistance in the preparation of this book.

🌷 A GOLDEN BOOK • NEW YORK

It is said that dogs are people's best friends. A dog can be a lot more than a friend, however. Sometimes a dog can be a lifesaving hero.

This is the tale of a brave dog named Balto. In 1925, he helped save a tiny community from a deadly disease.

The story begins in Nome, a frozen gold-rush town in Alaska. Nome was hundreds of miles from any big city. Deep snow and ice covered Nome in winter, and because there were no roads in the area, the only way to travel was by dogsled.

Drivers, or "mushers," and their dog teams often hauled supplies to gold-mining camps in wintertime. They also delivered mail all over Alaska. When mushers weren't working, they held races to see whose teams were the fastest.

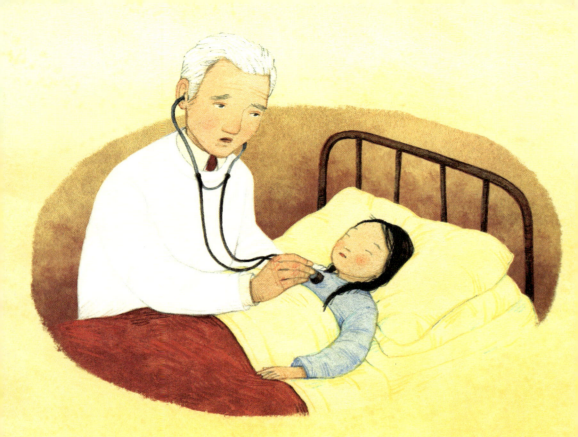

The Alaskan winter of 1925 was the coldest in twenty years. On January 21, Nome's only physician, Dr. Curtis Welch, got some terrible news. Two children were very sick with a deadly disease called diphtheria, and it was spreading fast.

The only cure was an antitoxin serum, but there wasn't enough serum in Nome to treat all who might need it. Without the medicine, the two children and others might die.

Dr. Welch learned that there were 300,000 doses of the serum in Anchorage. But Anchorage was more than 500 miles away. Could he have it delivered to Nome in time?

NOME

The doctor and the townspeople came up with a plan. The medicine would travel by train to the village of Nenana, 484 miles away. And there was only one safe way to get it from Nenana to Nome—by dog team.

NENANA

ANCHORAGE

A relay of twenty of the fastest teams was quickly
organized. Each team would carry the serum for one
leg of the journey.

The fastest a dog team had ever made the trip from
Nenana to Nome was nine days—but depending on
the weather, the trip could easily take three or four
weeks. If that happened, many more people in Nome
would get sick.

Gunnar Kaasen was a musher who was chosen for the relay. One of the dogs in his team was a Siberian husky named Balto.

Each team had a lead dog. The lead dog set the pace and kept the team on the trail. They had to be smart, strong, and able to respond quickly to the mushers' commands.

No one knew the trails better than a lead dog.

Racing over snow and ice could be very dangerous. Crossing frozen rivers and sea ice was even more dangerous. All drivers had heard about teams plunging through ice and disappearing forever.

Kaasen set out from Nome for a tiny village named Bluff. His team would carry the serum to Port Safety on the next-to-last leg of the relay.

Balto was not a lead dog at first. Kaasen saw something special in Balto, but he chose another dog to lead his team.

The serum arrived by train in Nenana on January 27. The package, covered in fur and canvas to keep it warm and dry, was swiftly loaded onto the first dogsled. There wasn't a moment to waste!

The first teams raced nonstop through snow and temperatures that were twenty degrees below zero for almost five days. Miraculously, all the dog teams reached their destinations.

The serum arrived in Bluff on February 1. Kaasen loaded it onto his sled as quickly as he could. "Mush!" he commanded, and the team of thirteen dogs raced off into the night.

Blinding snow and icy winds pummeled Kaasen and his team. At one point, the snow became so deep that the dogs nearly got buried. Some dogs howled with fright, but Balto stayed calm.

As Kaasen's team approached the village of Solomon, the lead dog stopped in his tracks. A second would-be lead dog did the same thing. Because of drifting snow, the two dogs could not locate the trail.

But Balto pulled against his harness and barked excitedly. He'd made this run many times! Since he seemed to know exactly where the trail was, Kaasen decided to try Balto in the lead dog position.

Meanwhile, back in Nome, the board of health sent
a telegram to Solomon, telling teams to wait out the
storm. They thought it was better to delay the delivery
than lose it.

But Kaasen never saw the telegram. And it was so dark outside, he didn't see Solomon. By the time he realized he'd driven past the village, he was already miles beyond it. So the team kept going.

Halfway across a frozen river, Balto stopped abruptly. Kaasen called, "Mush!" but Balto wouldn't move. Soon Kaasen realized why—the ice ahead was cracked! Balto had saved the team from falling into the icy water. They quickly found a safer path and continued on their journey.

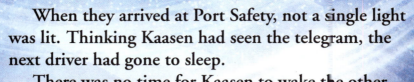

When they arrived at Port Safety, not a single light
was lit. Thinking Kaasen had seen the telegram, the
next driver had gone to sleep.

There was no time for Kaasen to wake the other
driver and load his sled. He and his dogs were
exhausted—but he decided to push on for the
last twenty miles to Nome.

With Balto in the lead, the team raced through the blizzard. There were times when Kaasen couldn't even see the trail. But Balto could.

Later that night, a fierce wind hit the sled and sent it flying. Kaasen was able to turn the sled upright, but when he looked for the medicine, it was gone!

Kaasen dug desperately in the snow. He finally found the package, and the team raced on through the night. At last, they pulled into Nome. Balto and the other twelve dogs on his team had run nonstop for twenty hours, covering fifty-three miles. Nome was saved!

Kaasen was hailed as a hero—but he said Balto was the real hero.

Balto's story made newspaper headlines across America, and he soon became a national sensation. He and the other dogs went on tour. A Hollywood movie was even made about Balto.

After the excitement wore off, however, the dogs ended up in a sideshow act in California. They did not do well there. The once-strong dogs became unhealthy.

A Cleveland, Ohio, businessman named George Kimball wanted to save the dogs and offered to buy them. But the price was $2,000—a huge sum at that time—so Kimball launched a fund-raising drive. Dog lovers across the country sent in their dimes and dollars. Children mailed their pennies to help the unhappy dogs.

The drive was a success! Kimball was able to bring Balto and the other dogs to the Cleveland Zoo, where they lived out their lives in comfort and thousands of fans could visit them.

There were, of course, other heroes in this famous story. Togo was lead dog for a driver named Leonhard Seppala. Togo and his team covered ninety-one miles, the longest leg of the relay, including a treacherous twenty miles over sea ice.

But it was Balto who captured the public's imagination. In New York City's Central Park, a statue was erected in 1925, the same year as that legendary Alaskan trek, to honor Balto and his team.

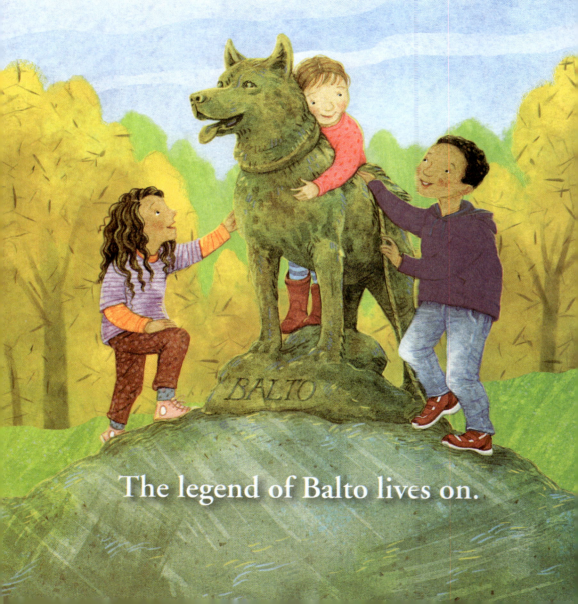

The legend of Balto lives on.